Shiva Dancing

poems by

Van Hartmann

texture press
2007

Shiva Dancing

poems by

Van Hartmann

Acknowledgments

"Aspens," "Driving South," "Old Bones," and "Prayers" appeared in *Red Wheelbarrow Magazine*
"The Cat" and "Totem" appeared in *Snake Nation*
"Eagle Eye" appeared in *Inkwell*
"Pelicans at Dawn" appeared in *Phi Kappa Phi Forum*
"Reunion" appeared in *The Worcester Review*
"Sequins" appeared in *Texas Review*
"The Watch" appeared in *Pennsylvania English*

Photographs of Warren Hartmann's wood carvings were taken by Jon Seaton and Patti Hartmann. Landscapes were photograph by Van Hartmann.

| ISBN 0-9797573-0-4 | ISBN13: 978-0-9797573-0-3 | Shiva Dancing |

Library of Congress Control Number: 207902755
First Edition © 2007 by Van Hartmann All Rights Reserved
cover art: Van Hartmann

Texture Press Guilderland, NY 12084
Managing Editor: Susan Smith Nash
Sales and Marketing: Elaine Bontempi

Sales and Marketing offices:
1108 Westbrooke Terrace
Norman, OK 73072
e-mail: texturepress@beyondutopia.com
phone: 405-314-7730

For

Roslyn Hartmann
(1945 - 2000)

and for

Warren Hartmann
(1914 - 2006)

Table of Contents

Old Bones	4
The Cat	5
Chaplains	7
Eagle Eye	9
Arranging Flowers	12
Ticks	13
Sunset without You	15
Pelicans at Dawn	17
Sequins	18
Power Lines	19
The Canoe	20
Aspens	22
Peeing	24
Running the Valley	26
Totem	34
The Watch	37
Mojave	41
Blue	42
Christmas Gifts	45
Matter	48
Splitting Maple	49
Mowing Lawns	50
Winter Squall	52
Reunion	53
One Low, Three High	56
Driving South	57
This New Window	58
Tennis in a Time of War	59
Prayers	61
Shiva Dancing	63
Here	67

Old Bones

My dog has buried bones that lie
forgot until a change of seasons
pushes up a scent through the moist earth
that snaps her head like a lead pulled tight.
Then she sets to digging, butt up,
paws and claws in furious excavation,
snout caked with mud, head
disappearing beneath the sod.

I've buried bits of you that molder
beneath the frost, sunk from sight
until I catch a hint of something past,
a strand of Shalimar
threading through a crowded room,
fragment of a face, echo of a laugh,
a long slow note extruded from a clarinet.

My digging sometimes yields
a hollow femur that settles
heavy on the spattered ground.
Sometimes I extract a memory
I can wrap again with flesh,
fill with breath, swell into a poem.

The Cat

Our cat emits a soft chatter,
tail twitching, limbs coiled, eyes nailed
to a chipmunk that meanders
beyond our bedroom window
feeding on sprigs of weed and grass.
The cat has stalked this prey
across the morning, racing
from room to room, bounding
from sill to sill, abruptly
crouching, deathly still,
plaster cast of itself,
silent except for the low whine
of primal gears that spin
in preparation for the instant
the screen might part
and it could spring,
a programmed arc of calico,
for the kill.

I will want the cat beside me
tonight in the cubicle that holds you,
where once again I'll watch the lines
meander blue and green, left to right
across your monitor, rapt
by that little dance of ions,
half believing some act of will
could force its hieroglyphic chaos
back to order.

But I can't pierce the mesh of gray
that falls across your face, nor grasp
the simple rodent fact,
the thing itself that moves within,
consuming organs, vessels, flesh,
your heart, your smile, your voice, your laugh.
For that I'll have to bring the cat
who's sat through eons
neither hopeful nor forlorn,
a softly humming statue
stalking death.

Chaplains

Every day they came
tapping at the door,
bony fingers gathered to a point,
like crows at dawn
years later cracking open
gray encrusted sleep,
pecking at the farmhouse window
where I would leave a bowl
of peanuts, some apples, and a peach,
night's unfinished feast,
on the white tiled counter,
spread before the flat black discs
blinking greedy snapshots
at the rich abundance
beyond the glass.

Like that they came, day after day,
until worn down you yielded.
In they fluttered,
soft voices, thin smiles
narrow little eyes,
to offer you a prayer.
You asked for something from the Torah.
Their heads bobbed
and met on tilted necks
then popped upright again.
We have just the perfect thing
they reassured,
smiling beatitudes in unison.
You opened if not to hope
then comfort,
raised your head above the dented pillow
and welcomed them
as one would welcome sunshine
into March.

Their bodies ruffled
huddled humbly smug
then intoned, *Our Father
who art in heaven*

hallowed be Thy name.
I saw your eyes glaze gray,
head drop and drift away,
heard you close yourself again,
more resigned than disappointed,
and if that
not so much in them,
just a couple in a flock of crows
come pecking for your soul,
as in the opaque vision
the glass gave back,
life's blank indifference
self-involved, moving past.

As for them,
they fluttered out again,
fat on golden peanuts
crammed in beaks
and mouths, they thought,
dripping sweet juices
of apple and peach.

Eagle Eye

Eagle eye, you called yourself, and beamed
rainbows when you mastered every letter
on the chart at the DMV
and the little man with glasses
noted that your sight
was better than twenty-twenty.
Neither pennies nor insects escaped your scrutiny.
God knows how many times I climbed
a ladder to squash an errant bug.
You marked the blots I missed on countertops,
found wayward pens, proofread
my dissertation, saw the flaws
in seams and fabrics on slacks
and shirts I almost bought.
When we drove from Carolina to New York,
you scanned the shoulders, shouting "Furry!"
at each waddling woodchuck by the way.

When the computer monitor at work
began to take its toll, you fretted.
Then came the morphine.
Your vision went berserk.
Fractured plates, sprouting plants, faces
long forgot began to crowd the room,
and you and I despaired
of ever having faith in sight again.

But when you saw your dead daddy
waiting by our bedroom door
I knew you were onto something
even eagles couldn't see.
I smoothed your brow and pulled your lids shut
over those two rivets, talons,
greedy for that image in their grasp.

Arranging Flowers

Roses were the worst,
tight buds,
layered embellishments,
unreliable narratives
that opened, darkened, fell away.

On the third day you didn't rise again,
but the flowers began to stink.

My advice is,
next time you die,
start simple.
Pick a batch of daffodils
yourself
somewhere at the meadow's edge
very early in the morning
while it still receives the shadow of the woods
before word gets out
that you are ill.
In the evening, discard them.
Start again next morning
very early.
Repeat this every day through eternity.

Ticks

Picking ticks from Phoebe's fur
– we'd just returned from walking to the bay,
taking in the swath of silver thread
the morning sun had cut across the water –
your sister told of Sunshine's death,
that big blonde standard who stalked you playfully,
then pounced as you retreated laughing,
but half afraid the ancient wolf
would wake and lunge in earnest.
The moment Sunshine died, ticks ran off,
brown flood flowing from his golden carcass,
mute Diaspora, scrambling into cracks and crannies,
clotting walls, waiting for some hot and bloody thing
to pass that way again.

That was your sister's story.

Mine lies in a yellow folder clogged with sheets,
on each your name, date of birth,
date and cause of death.
I've spent the morning calling offices, agencies,
all polite, efficient, sorry for my loss.
I never knew how valuable you were.
Everywhere I find a benefit, policy,
check to be issued on receipt
of one of those certificates.
I sit addressing envelopes,
wolfish, bloodstained, ticks thin with thirst
rattling in the cabinet. I send them out,
despite my urge to shut the drawer,
lock it tight, like the sealed urn
in which I placed your ashes.

Piece by piece you're carried off,
leaving cold remains,
bones of memories:
our final walk along the beach;
a silver thread laced with pink
slipped silent from the corner of your mouth.

Sunset without You

I think Kandinsky scored this evening's sky.
Swallows, dusky brown, spiral
across bouquets of lava, burgundy, peach;
a symphony of flight
caresses the spreading night.
Shadows fall
and rise on currents
beyond my reach;
particles of darkness
tug at me to take a turn
on silent spinning notes.

The dog, sure-footed,
barks and chooses land.
For the best part of the dying hour
her yellow form sweeps the green field
harvesting light,
a metronome swung urgently
from tuft to tuft as the sun drops
scale by scale, until she stops, turns,
hurries to my call,
fixing me in time and place.

But I can feel Kandinsky's brush.
The sky churns with music.
Night approaches.
I ache to hear the song
that makes the swallows dance.

Pelicans at Dawn

A strand of pelicans glides along the surf,
fifteen, eighteen, maybe twenty black pearls
strung across the sky,
growing quickly into chunks
of slate sliding over slate,
stones flung low against the dawn,
leaden, large, improbable,
refusing to drop, rocking
from side to side, lifting, lilting,
riding the draft that glances off the swell;
between their dark plumage
and the murmuring sea
a thin crease of morning light,
like a door left slightly ajar.

They whisper to me
in their silent flight
that all that was lost
during the previous night
might find its way back
through that slender space.
Then one of them veers, hooked
it would seem, by a line from the deep,
plummets, then surfaces, glistening and sleek,
something dying clamped in its beak.

Sequins

Today I took the dog to search for you
along the path we walked last winter
in that brief lull between the storms
and recalled the lines you loved
from Doty's poem, "no such thing,
the queen said, as too many sequins."
As the dog and I approached the sign
that always made you stop and do the bump,
because, you said, that's what it said to do,
a gust of autumn wind engulfed a grove
of nearby elms and gave them such a shake
they rained a shower of
amber, crimson, emerald, gold.
The dog went wild chasing bits of fractured light.
I almost heard you laugh. Outrageous, you,
who once picked up your wine and placed it
briefly on the table next to you
because the pill you had to take
said "do not mix with alcohol."
Undaunted, you who told the hospice nurse
you had to walk because you knew
that if you stopped you'd die,
and so, like tireless Hobson in Milton's poem,
you walked and walked and walked
until the nurse gave up all hope
of laying you discreetly to your rest.

Then you stopped. Rude impossibility.
You whose laugh could crack apart
the morning sky became a silence
full of sequins, missing everywhere.

Power Lines

On its southern flank the cherry tree
surprises me with buds,
greening branches bobbing over power lines,
young girls in early spring, hint of nipples and hips,
mastering double-dutch and hopscotch,
beneath the bark a pulse pushing toward summer.
But its north side continues leafless,
gray trunk tattered with ragged stubs,
beset by bracket fungi,
the ground beneath littered with limbs.
I worry about the wires that weave
through the forest, fret over filaments
soon to be engulfed by that rotting tree,
know I should report it,
bring a band of brawny men
armed with cables, cleats, and saws
that keen like crones, protect the fragile threads
that tie this silent house to the present.

I summon you contracted into gray,
inside, a green girl wanting to skip,
hot current pulsing through your hazel eyes.
Beset by tubes that kept you tethered
to a metal pole on wheels that tilted
precariously, you named it Romero,
called him your dance partner,
cast a sly grin, wove your tendril arms
through plastic coils, dipped and spun
a Lindy through your final winter.

The Canoe

Today, I sold your blue Volkswagen
to a nice law student, a kid
you would have flirted with,
then found for him a girl
who wouldn't mind his acne.
I caught him smirking to his friend,
brought to test the brakes, steering, shocks;
you'd think he'd won his first case,
the way he rushed to seal the deal with cash.

I didn't tell him the car was haunted,
nor disclose how hard it's been to extract
your remains from among the brake fluid,
oil, ice scrapers, coolant,
handiwipes, quarters, and rags,
provisions packed for the journey
you knew you'd someday take.

It caught you unawares.
How else explain the satin sequined chili peppers
left to dangle from the rearview mirror?
Or the trunk's lingering scent of saddle,
chaps and crop, braided handle
worn smooth by your grip;
helmet, black and dusty, curry comb,
half a box of biscuits for the spaniels at the stable.

Buried deeper, the folding nylon chair,
blue blanket, red towel for that spot on the Sound
you shared with me after you fell sick
and could only walk short distances,
pulling me through razor grass and spartina
to a small cove of white sand and turquoise ocean
smelling of salt and drying kelp,
offered with halting steps, as if confessing covert sin,
harbored secrets, carefully concealed plans for departure.

I told none of this to the law student,
nor how I'd kept the thing tethered
against a year of currents,

how you rode the clutch, tended to tailgate,
about the time you tried to embark again
during your short recovery,
thinking you knew at last the schedule and the route,
ignored my warnings,
shot the car through pitch black night,
onto an unmarked asphalt curb.

Instead, I emptied the trunk,
hung the chili peppers like amulets
from the mirror of my new Subaru,
took the cash, whispered a blessing
as your car slid slowly into traffic,
freed from its mooring,
a blue canoe laden with your spirit,
paddled by unwitting priests.

Aspens

We rode single file, climbing sheets of rock
on slender equine limbs, thin air
stealing our breath, plumes of smoke
exhaling from the creatures' nostrils;
saddles creaked and lurched,
hooves struck a muffled beat against the stone,
lulling us as the lake sank
to a silver pebble a thousand feet below.
You were the better rider,
freer to feel your horse's muscles between your thighs,
freer to inhale the cold smell of the mountain;
I see it on your face in the photograph.

You looked up first when the ridge broke open
to expose a sunlit grove of swaying aspens,
bark crudely carved, black hieroglyphs
on white papyrus, or hollow painted poles
in which Aborigines bury their dead,
except these rustled, shimmered,
angered me to find graffiti
in this wild abandoned place.
Our guide explained that shepherds
working flocks left messages
for each other and themselves.

"Where do they go?" you asked me.
"Most have probably died."
"No, the messages, in the winter
when the mountains fill with snow
and no one can read them.
Do they still whisper?"
"I don't know," I answered.
"Someday the snow will cover me," you said.
"and you will have to brush it off to read my name."

Peeing

My colleague said his grandson
stopping in the woods to pee
let loose an arc
that scattered leaves, furrowed ground,
swept away a line of marching ants;
when finished,
zipped his jeans, resumed their hike
as if it were a normal boy's
normal thing to pee like this
walking through the forest.

We marveled, old men
sharing old men's secrets,
tending to rituals of the urinal,
attentive to drips, leaks, spots,
darkened tendrils spreading down
the fronts of khaki trousers.

Later,
I recalled the catheter between your legs,
face plastered flat by fear
you'd never pee again,
then heard you weeping wonder
when they took it out,
bed pan sounding
like the porch roof under summer rain,
hoarded treasure newly coined
cascading down a wishing well
dug too soon too deep.

Running the Valley

Last night my father asked me
to teach him long division.
The question swept away the Ark
he helped me frame from boyhood
sitting at our kitchen table
tutoring geometry and calculus,
sharing fragments of work
on missiles and gears,
debating God,
teasing out the thin thread
between belief and doubt.
I wanted to cover his shame,
but feared he'd strike me blind
for seeing his nakedness.

This morning I take to the pavement,
running this route the first time since your death,
feet pounding out an argument
sharp and brittle like the tendons in my knees,
flee across a landscape of flood and thirst,
a Santa Ana ricocheting down
the southern slope of the Santa Susana,
reminding me of the windstorm
that nearly swept us off the road
in Mojave the summer after our wedding.
Step after step, I stab at the past,
retrace the loop we mapped together
two years ago when we thought he was dying,
running west up Victory, past Berquist,
past the house where my French teacher lived,
past Lederer and Platt,
where we paused for the light,
up that gentle incline to Valley Circle Drive,
turning north, passing Spanish workers
huddled amid ice plant and ivy
in the shade of an adobe wall,
bent against the wind, bearing the curvature
of Oaxaca or Quito or San Salvador.
Ahead, in the low angle of the early sun
we saw an aged Asian man

gather olives beneath a tree,
dip and sway as if to trace
some ancient rite; we laughed,
remembering the Chinese couple
we'd pass in Chapel Hill
who broke into calisthenics
whenever they saw us approaching.
This year the olives have been gleaned,
my knees rebel against the asphalt,
the wind snaps at my chest like parchment.

The leg up Valley Circle continues
for a mile, still rising; across the road
enormous houses spawn on rolling hills
where avocado groves once grew,
but that brown mass of rock I used to climb
with boyhood friends still stands,
deep inside, the dank recess of Bat Cave
where slippery shadows creased the dark.
You asked, wasn't I afraid of snakes;
we recalled the photo you took
returning from the beach, late one afternoon,
me barefoot, top of Topanga,
striking a pose between a cliff and a pile of leaves
that stirred into a rattlesnake.

At the crest, I turn east onto Vanowen,
still pushing at the wind, but dropping
toward the valley floor, back across Platt,
passing more workers clustered listless in the rising heat.
It was here I began to lengthen my stride,
thighs contracting, expanding, smooth and rhythmic,
lungs and heart finding their pace, knees fluid,
feet digging up rivulets from the past.
On the right lived a girl I asked for a date;
ahead, the home of a friend
who picked up a policeman's wife
one night while we were bowling,
told me how she'd take him in her mouth
after making love to get him hard again,
how one afternoon she started crying and couldn't stop.

I stretch my sight to the valley's end,
draw a bead across the mountains,
through the wind that blows off the Mojave,
over the Rockies, past the plains,
reverse the route my parents took
in a green Plymouth with three kids
and a black spaniel, slide on
across the sluggish Mississippi,
yet farther back to a musty barn
on an autumn night, southwest Ohio,
me ten, Nita thirteen, fresh
from Florida with tits and the jitterbug,
daughter of the woman my best friend's father
brought home to replace his wife who,
dying from cancer, called me to her bed
and, taking my hand in her thin hot grasp,
said goodbye in a whisper as brittle as straw.
Nita later took my hand,
led me up a set of wooden steps
to the loft above the backboard
where her new brother and I shot baskets,
unzipped the zipper of her boy's jeans
amid the pine beams and fresh hay
and beckoned me in vain.

I see my father in full Midwestern summer
wielding the wide flat disk of a rotary mower,
cropping the front field like a crew cut,
preparing to till and plant,
smell of earth and grass and sweat
taking seed in my memory.
I turn south onto Woodlake,
now flowing toward home.
The whine of the rotor slips to a rhythmic slosh;
he works a wide hoe through a shallow sluice
of wet concrete, my brother and I measuring
careful scoops of heavy powder from a gray bag,
our father's back leaning and pulling against
the thickening weight of western heat,
the ground partitioned by redwood rails,
a gaping grid waiting to be filled, leveled, and set.

Then I stumble,
thinking how two years ago
I'd left you far behind,
and almost turn to look for you.
You linger locked in our first night,
dancing to Aretha Franklin,
Dorton Arena, Raleigh, North Carolina,
your ticket saved all these years
beneath a magnet on the refrigerator door,
you folding me into yourself
against a frozen February
that erupted into summer,
you running ripe and wet,
nectarine, pomegranate, peach,
face flushed, eyes fathomless, greedy, feral,
we riding each other,
predator and prey, teeth, saliva, claws,
building storm, cloudburst, levees collapsing,
I hanging on for dear life,
earth and time and space dissolving,
we dissolving, becoming nothing,
lifeless, inert, lost amid humus and flood.
Slowly we awakened to drift along the aftermath,
crisscrossed limbs stirring languidly,
fingers tentatively tracing tendons and veins,
blindly reconstructing eyelids, cheekbones,
chins, the lines of noses and lips,
silently mapping the miracle
of our spent and sated bodies,
taking each other's measure,
setting the standard against which
all that followed would fail,
ebb and flood of a marriage
awash in fragments of memory.

I falter, see you broken,
exuding fluids from fistulas;
like Blake's Ancient of Days
I spread compasses, calipers,
plot the input and output
of your body's effluvia
in gradated vials and charts,

wrap measuring tape thrice daily
around your edematous legs,
carefully record the inches
as they swell into shapelessness,
madly try to keep you meaningful and whole,
you struggling merely to remember
your only sister's telephone number,
at the end, all of life's unknowable oceans
contracted into that one tear
that clung mute and indecipherable
to your hot cheek the morning you died.

I could drown in that tear.

But the wind slaps at my back,
hot, insistent, pushing me forward.
Turning west onto Victory,
I see my parents' lawn,
once a carpet of dichondra,
the walnut trees across the street
fallen to tract homes long before I met you.
My father and you work crossword puzzles
at the kitchen table, laughing;
then you stand beside me
at the door to the den, my mother
across the room, folded numb and mute,
preparing for grief,
paramedics calling out measurements,
blood pressure, pulse, teasing him back to life.
You command me in a whisper to go to her.

I need you now to tell me
how to face an old man
chanting memories like mantras,
trying to hold and order his past.
I listen for your whisper.
Perhaps I hear it beneath my feet
helping me make my argument,
helping me build my Ark,
telling me to go to the table
where he sits waiting
for me to teach him his math,

there to take the measure
of how many times
each of you goes into my life.

Totem

Grandfather lost his index finger
pounding out a carpenter's wage
across Wyoming, Utah, Montana,
hammering, planing, sanding
shelves of ash to shine
like fields of wheat, making mahogany
slide beneath his thumb like a worn penny.
He hefted tools from town to town,
waiting for the boom to bust before
seeing a doctor about the sliver
of pine that defied his digging
with the pocket knife
he'd carried since he was twelve.
He was sullen when I knew him,
spent his days haunting entryways
to factories, woodshops, train yards,
mumbling, pointing with his stub,
surveying other men's work,
compulsively consulting a gold watch
he'd bought with his first month's pay.

Sometimes I take that watch from its glass case,
compress the catch to feel the precision
with which its cover springs open
between forefinger and thumb,
only to find grandfather's jealous eye
staring out at me.

My father's hands caned chairs
in even shuttle motions,
tapping tight the fibers into solid mats.
At night at the kitchen table
he chiseled blocks of avocado
into human figures.
On June Lake in the Sierra
he baited hooks, untangled reels,
fingers numbed by mountain cold,
slid a knife precisely down the bellies
of trout from anus to throat, followed
with his thumb, scooping out organs and gore.

Those hands planted trees, mixed concrete,
set cinder blocks in place, tamped them level,
grooved the space between
to build the wall around our yard.

Beyond that wall, he seldom let me see
the hands at work for forty years
drawing gears, guidance systems,
missiles, rockets, bombs, dark compromise
for our suburban California home.

I have a gymnast's hands, shaped
by handstands, handsprings, ropes, and bars
that raised my veins like blue highways.
I took my turn at carving wood,
then twisted wire into little sculptures.
But once I tore the tendons
on the index finger of my right hand,
saw it dangle limp and useless,
a dead trout, and felt grandfather's eye
surveying me from toe to crown.
And once a woman from rural Carolina,
reading the lines that mapped my calloused palms,
stopped abruptly, left the room distressed.
Now I carve totems out of words
and listen for a gold watch ticking in its tomb.

The Watch

My grandfather hadn't much to give,
didn't know how to give it:
box of aging tools with drawers
of blades and bits and chisels,
carpenter's clamps with sliding brackets
that could have squeezed the Devil out of witches;
stub of a missing finger, false teeth
that floated on a thin pool of brown
tobacco juice, German name of Karl
discarded during the War;
heart clenched like a walnut shell
around a marriage compressed
to bickering and skirmishes.
Not much for a kid like me;
worst of all, a knee
that demanded sitting on,
while his damaged grasp
clamped like a rusted vise
onto my skinny arm.

I made the best of every visit,
gave a smile for a penny,
laugh for a nickel,
almost anything to wriggle free
from his four fingered claw,
breath of cheap cigars,
old man smell of his knitted vest.
But he'd cling to me,
occasional cackle erupting
through his gums because
my middle name was Charles,
and someone had finally
named someone after him.
Eventually, a long chain
would snake out of a hidden pocket.
A gold watch dangled before my eyes.
He'd pop it open, grunt, release me
with a sigh, and off I'd go.

When he had his heart attack,

he left me the watch,
an Elgin, fitting solid in my palm,
each side elegantly engraved
with lines that fanned out
from tiny ovals near the hinge,
one filled with little petals,
the other left bare, awaiting
initials or a name never entered,
an heirloom, my father told me,
a working man's first investment,
after his tools, a piece of crafted gold
to last a lifetime, or several.

A jeweler soon destroyed that claim.
Gold filled, not eighteen carats,
obvious from the guarantee,
Good for twenty years,
stamped inside the cover.
Still, it's held up well, considering.
Runs slow, though, no fixing that,
timing holes worn out.

Even with its gears recalibrated,
missing second hand
and broken cover spring replaced,
it's a curious contraption
full of gaps and slippages,
little silver solar systems
spinning carelessly,
planets inside of planets
running retrograde,
missing deadlines, extending visits,
playing havoc with schedules.
But at my age I like the way it shuts
like Grandfather's hand on my wrist,
devil of a grip, lasting a lifetime.

Mojave

My father's eyes have lost their center,
macula crumbling cell by cell,
drying the core to which his world is rooted,
leaving fleeting glimpses caught obliquely,
collapsing like his memory.
He watches television staring at the closet door,
looks for my face in my left shoulder.

To see him scan a room
reminds me of a sandstorm
once that flung shotgun blasts of sand and grit
against my windshield, pitting it opaque.
When evening came, approaching beams
refracted rainbows through the speckled glass.

We know light bends,
pulled in a tug of war
between gravity and dark matter.
The Master, conversing with the Old One,
saw it in his lab, that domed desert
where each of us will end,
the center of his own narration,
narrow polished pane of fact
dissolving into story.

Blue

For weeks he's brooded over Blue,
the missing jay he trained
to take a peanut from his hand,
afraid the mocking birds or crows chased it off,
or it was a victim of the drought,
or the neighbor's cat finally killed it.

In its absence light has seeped
out of the center of things,
leaving holes where he leans to try to see
a page, a face, a TV screen.
Hearing has failed him too,
casting him adrift in muttered memories:
how at ten he strapped two slats to his feet,
skied down hills in Snyder Park;
at twenty, rebuilt a four-stroke Indian Scout,
raced his friends through winding roads;
at forty, told a bastard boss to screw himself,
took the job that brought our family west,
read Albert Schweitzer, gave his twenty gauge away;
crafted furniture from avocado, oak, and ash,
poured this patio, raised these walls,
planned to build a sailboat with his sons.

During these dark weeks
he's shuffled from chair to chair,
growing fretful, earth-inclined,
his liturgy sinking to lament:
the alleyway is choked
with graffiti, trash, and predators;
his sons went off to college and never returned;
the center where his blood gets cleaned
is full of Filipinos
who talk in Spanish behind his back;
the long corroding illnesses
of friends have made him wish
he hadn't brought us kids into the world;
if something happened to our mother
he'd never let us put him in a home,
but use the thirty-eight with the walnut stock

he carved himself and the stash of bullets
he's hidden in the garage.

Blue came back today,
threaded sunlight from the power line
to the mulberry branch,
strung a lei to the lemon tree,
and landed on my father's outstretched palm.
The old man smiles at the patio's edge,
balancing precariously
beneath the weight of a bird
and a peanut shell,
pausing
between gravity and air.

Christmas Gifts

When younger than I am now
he'd carved the walnut stock
with his own hands
and showed it to me once,
pulling it from where it lay beneath
a mound of memories in a drawer –
cold resolve he hid
against the fate he saw unfolding.

Now time was past
when he could hold the threatened thirty-eight
against his muddled temple,
or sign the card we bought at Eckerd's
with the cheap perfume, L'Air du Temps,
and Neil Diamond compact disc
my mother said was all she wanted,
making sure she slipped some twenties in his wallet.
He laid a couple softly on the counter,
smoothing each like blind Tireseas
spreading entrails,
scanning clues to where he'd been,
where his mind would wander next,
but grounded briefly in that simple task
of counting, touch, and texture,
and the slowly hatching prospect –
held as one would hold a still wet feathered thing
quivering in its freshly fractured shell –
of giving gifts
pulled from his own pockets.

His face would tangle later
as he asked
if he got a present yet for Mother,
then touch two fingers to his temple,
divining something brooding deep within,
watch me flounder across
a several-thousand-year-old stream
of prophecy and taboo to write
as if in his own hand,

*To my dearest wife, with all my love,
from your devoted husband, Warren.*

Matter

I see his eyesight failing
in this one's flattened cheekbones,
that one's smile contorted to a smirk,
the way the spotted dog
on the bookshelf there
against its master's knee
has its canine point
embarrassed to a boxy snout.

He freed a flock of seagulls once,
let new wings spread
from chunks of avocado
into freshly opened
paths of air.
For years they flew
above our mantle,
twisting pulsing honey grain
released by chisels
from deep inside a block of wood.

He grew angry toward the end
when matter clotted sight,
thickened fingers,
shut his breath in weakened caves
of air compressing flesh
until at last it rolled
a stone of phlegm
against the pathway out.

Now no art can carve away
that stone, no tools can lift
his bones to air and light.

Splitting Maple

I've heard men say it's best
to split your hardwood freshly cut.
These logs have lain from fall to fall,
less time than those my father
seasoned, links of avocado, tulip, bass,
when he had eyes to work a chisel
at their grain.
I raise the maul, pause for aim,
let gravity suck its thick gray head to earth.
The iron recoils against the spongy stone.

I turn one on its end,
wonder what carved figure it might make,
but find the line between
the cloven tree and moist earth
dissolved to something porous,
dissolute, as if the soil were rising
to invade what once was hers.
Centipedes, slugs, things unseen
boring tiny veins
have recreated Eden
in the footprint of a log.

How quick the earth takes back her own,
unless I intercede,
keeping flesh from sinking back to flesh,
splitting wood for winter,
carving fallen fathers into gods.

Mowing Lawns

My father taught me to mow
in straight swaths like a tailor
laying out a fabric of green
herring bone in alternating weave.
Set a plan and follow it.
Don't meander across the landscape
leaving ragged tufts and ugly seams.
Options were limited.
Shave close the overlap, eliminate a pass.
Begin adjacent to the garage,
draw lanes the length of the lawn,
up and back, up and back,
doing kick turns at each end,
spreading a flat wake across the yard
with the slowly moving morning sun.
Or, start on the circumference,
heading either left or right, then pivot
ninety degrees right or left at each corner
with increasing frequency,
running around a shrinking track,
arriving finally at a small top knot,
green and silly at the center,
then with the mower slice it off.

His method served me well,
left a satisfying scent of cut grass,
gave heft to a boy
mastering a man's craft, prepared me
for later skills: how to hit a nail square;
hold a shotgun, swing and pull;
hang a door, raise a joist, frame a window,
plot a path through life.

But if I had a son,
I'd take him to the meadow,
show him doves in flight,
starlings circling home at night,
take him to the ocean,
plot the paths of bluefish, spots, and cod,
find a prairie,

watch the bison graze in slow meander,
follow squirrels working autumn ground,
read him *Tristram Shandy*, Whitman, Hopkins, Joyce,
set him loose and hope
he'd leave that little clump of daisies
or wild oregano intact,
or maybe mow his name into the grass.

Winter Squall

It starts as little notes
dropped carelessly,
an F, an E, a random C,
drifting down the clef of clouds
someone's drawn against the day;
curvature of cellos, violas, violins
ripples through my hair;
bassoons, trombones, and oboes
blow about my face;
suddenly, a symphony
with kettledrums and blinding swirls
reorganizes land and space, withdraws
the line between the earth and sky,
sends me tumbling down a melody,
then just as sudden stops.

White remains begin to melt,
footprints vanish with the snow,
trace of a tune I find it hard to hum,
but recently did know.

Reunion

She had come to hate this photograph,
of him at Sanibel smiling his white-sand,
wave-breaking smile, face burnished and glowing,
balding crown radiating spokes of light,
chance trick of the camera, but catching,
they agreed, the truth he felt,
calling her manna, nectar, his burning bush;
he stood at ease in his wilderness,
white hair matted against his tanned chest,
hands on hips, elbows akimbo,
from the ankles up, the crease of his khakis
sharp as a seagull's cry, the bottoms
rolled, bunched, and wetted brown like kelp,
having arrived at this brief oasis
half cocky, half supplicating, somewhat
bemused to be again among the living,
fleshing out the frame of bone that lay
for weeks like a beached, storm-shattered hull.

She could have chosen others she hated
as much: moments congealing to a gelatin
through which he slowly sank,
a winter fish growing turgid in a frozen pond,
clouded, receding, descending into lies.
But this was the lie she had chosen.
Now she sat on this dark stretch of northern track,
having fluttered home, her instinct powerful and sure,
clutching the image, perched between the rails.

She felt as much as heard his voice approaching,
faint at first, a slowly swelling symphony;
salmon spawning on distant rivers,
tumbling up cataracts, falling back,
breaking through again, their thrashings
rolling down the mountain canyons;
she whispered back – nectar, manna –
then heard the roar of the surf, deep in the distance,
but growing; then the groan of wind parting water,
his voice now a storm arriving
like the rising of a thousand cranes.

Suddenly, out of the blank black slate of night,
his burnished face, a white and howling sun.

One Low, Three High

They drop by the wayside,
grandparent, neighbor,
mother of a childhood friend,
uncle, cousin, parent,
wife,
until we come to see
that we've no business here
stringing out our journey home
pausing at gravesides and weddings;
except there's a bird
that sings from the woods –
one low, three high,
one low, three high –
chanting its matins,
culling dark from light.

Driving South

The night before we left, a storm
dropped powder on the mountain to the west,
laying down a pall so fine that
in the morning sun a thick white cloud
seemed to settle on the forest,
as though angel's down and linen robes
had come to wrap us for the journey home.

You said, but this is nothing,
I should have seen the sunrise,
pink and gold and pebbled
mounds of pearls piled against the eastern sky.

On the drive south, the snow gave way
to crystal forests, Chilluly chandeliers,
brittle limbs and fingers of blown glass
tossing bits and fragments of fractured light
from mirror to mirror, savage beauty
of fire and ice so fragile
it could shatter to the touch.

Then, we rounded a curve
and entered a matted pelt of twigs,
carcass hill of brown,
mere bones of dormant trees.

You told me not to worry,
you saw the sunrise and all its pearls.
You're holding them for me.

This New Window

This new window
doesn't frame the Sound,
its clamshell moldings
land bound.
I see you through it
just the same
if I catch my lamp
at a certain glance
at three or four a.m.

It frames your face
within its glass,
sharp as dreams
before we wake.
Sometimes it pulls
nature out of joint;
fat moths, mosquitoes,
unnamed things
bouncing out of night
bombard the pane,
some seeking blood,
some seeking light,
incessant clatter,
slapping at the shore.

Tennis in a Time of War

A rectangle thirty-six by seventy-eight,
lined in unforgiving boxes
demarcates the boundaries
in which the yellow ball must fall,
a little world within the world,
mathematically precise, to which a dance
of angles, arcs, curves, and spins gives life;
and passion – sudden bursts of anger,
little wars of points won and points lost,
challenged calls, contested lines,
a racket flung, a curse;
but in the end the boundaries recomposed,
the court swept clean, the warriors reconvened
for pizza, beer, friendly cheer, a weekly world
from which we watch the larger one
contract in hatred, death, and fear.

There a foot fault means a severed leg,
a lob, a mortar or grenade
spinning out a calculus
that shreds a chest, removes an arm;
there passion bursts in howls and grunts,
the wail of some man's daughter
searching for her missing hand,
her melted wedding band;
there the court is swept by thick sand
that blows across the centuries
piling hatred into dunes,
clotting the Euphrates,
then sweeping round the world,
working through the cracks in our souls,
coating us with complicity.

I see you sitting on the bench
by the court they said you couldn't enter:
Players Only, no spouses, friends,
spectators, and certainly not
the dying. So we suited you up
in a purple nylon running shell that hung
from your bones like a becalmed spinnaker,

and white Etonics that barely closed
around the edema of your feet,
sat you down to watch with oscillating eyes
and a smile that argued pleasure at our folly.

You've come back in this time of war
bemused that we still work
so hard at our play
in these boxes inside of boxes,
this game inside a game,
this dance inside a dance,
knowing with a wisdom withheld
from those who haven't stood within
the hollow core from which exploded
endless waves of outward-hurtling husks,
our court is traced across a multitude of veils,
we surf a cosmic wind of dark matter,
the shadow ball at which we slap
is neither in nor out, the lines
are ever moving, the game is never won
nor lost, neither here nor in the desert.

Prayers

I cannot pray to God;
my mouth fills with bone and ash.
I think I can pray to the soft patina of snow
that set the world aglow,
as I walked home from her bed
at three this morning.
I pray that it smoothes the brow
of your grave, waters your dust,
cools your fever,
and flake by downward drifting flake
wraps my grief in silence.
I think I was praying
when I sank my lips
between her white thighs.
I prayed again, to you,
when I lay awake,
the new angles of her body
awkward against mine,
where yours once fit,
asking perhaps permission,
or grace.
And having come home
to the dog who has grown large
from the puppy I gave you,
I think my letting it use its bulk
to pull me out again into the falling snow
before I settle at last into my bed, our bed,
is a prayer.

Shiva Dancing

Our plane slid down the Hudson,
at the mouth, banked east,
its shadow traversing Manhattan,
shrinking, expanding, breaking into fragments
on roofs and sides of buildings,
then settled on a crevice
where it seemed a tooth had been extracted
from the city's jaw.

A year before, the wreckage still exhaled
an acrid breath; smoke and ash and swirling cells
spun a savage dance;
air was thick with supplication
for one more gasp, touch,
chance to ask forgiveness;
mingled whispers, muted howls
rose in dark plumes from the hollow throat.
Now, from half a mile above I gawked
dumbly at the remnants of their passion.

At LaGuardia, baggage, bustle, embraces
brushed away the shadow that briefly touched their dust.
You weren't there to greet me,
having passed through your own catastrophe
a full year earlier than theirs.
I knew that time was slipping forward,
the present pressing on the past,
relentless, indifferent, like Merrill's torn up block,
the massive volume of the world
closing shut again, even on our grief.

Now more years have crumbled.
I strain to see your face
through the ash and dust that you've become.

It was springtime,
that morning you lay dying.
A college festival outside our window
brought a brightly colored balloon filled with heat
that rose and fell in a nearby field;

shadows danced across the grass
from laughing students a hundred feet above the ground.
You had had a dying night,
shredded lungs and ragged breath
subsiding to a silent fever;
you wanted water desperately
but had no voice to ask.
The morning clouded up and rained,
which stilled the balloon but did you little good.
I wet a cloth, laid it on your forehead,
squeezed moisture from a dropper
to clear your clouding eyes,
soaked a sponge-tipped stick,
swabbed your mouth, and talked
to keep you tethered to the earth.

It was the sponge that held you.
On that you wrapped your tongue
and clamped your teeth so tight
I had to use some strength to extract it.
You clung to water at the end.
I left the room for one brief chore;
you drifted free.
When I returned your face was bent
to where I'd sat.
Red laced saliva slid onto the pillow.
A single tear wet your cheek.

Your fleeing molecules left a hole
that lay agape, dark matter
whispered into my nights.
I took to sleeping in the space you left behind,
trying to use my bulk to hold ajar
the door through which you departed.

But inexorably it closes.
Who can build a monument
sufficient to what we want:
the breath of their desire,
the grip of teeth on moistened sponges?
Instead, we're left to imagine them
from shadows left behind.

We'd like to think they've mingled in a graceful
minuet with those whose anguish
came before and after. We'd like to think
they fill a universe of particles
that gyrate in counterpoint to ours.
We try to picture Shiva dancing
madly in love with them, tossing
their fragments about the heavens,
preparing them for our reunion.
But we move on to others
who embrace us at airports,
help rebuild our homes.

What is this tale I'm telling you
who have no ears to hear?
A slim wedge I've set against
the volume of the world,
a little dance of images,
a fragile house of words.

Here

The here-ness of a thing
as it gathers late light,
oak leaves clumping green
against the slipping sky,
branches crusted thick with bark,
me now at summer's end,
eyes gleaning sun soaked fact,
stocking up for winter:
painful ripeness of a peach;
killdeer glinting white and tan and black
carving arcs across the switch;
horse flanks slick with lather,
hooves pawing at the edge of autumn,
nostrils working at the coming chill;
and tomorrow, little Max,
three years old, lives next door,
sisters heading off to school,
tilting on the topmost step,
blond mop head
spilling morning light,
shouting down, *Wait for me!*

"A Van Hartmann poem is a Van Hartmann poem. He doesn't remind us of anyone. When he shares a recollection, it is in bas-relief, and we are allowed the tactile surge that comes with precious few poems of the day. Keats would cherish these works, but not Byron; Jeffers, but not Spender. Hardy would pin them to his walls, for these poems have an extraordinary life force that convinces us–without sermon or anything remotely approaching self-pity or self-congratulation–that a compendium of recollected moments is joyously capable, in time, of partially warding off the crippling finality of loss."
    -Dan Masterson, author of *All Things, Seen and Unseen*, editor of *Enskyment.org*

"Shiva Dancing is an extraordinary first collection. The refreshing immediacy of Hartmann's voice, at times elegiac, resonates with complexities that comprise the mysteries of everyday life. Graceful syntactical structures create a varied, subtle music that best support the emotional depth of each narrative. As the title implies, loss is a constant theme and for the poet, as well as the reader, some form of redemption is found in poem after poem."
    -Kevin Pilkington, author of *Ready to Eat the Sky*

"With poetic skill, artful expression and honest insight, Van Hartmann confronts the loss that comes with living. This is a fine collection, one that matters, rich with sweet and sad poems. I read it with admiration and joy. You should read it, too." Mark DeFoe, author of *The Rock and the Pebble*.

Van Hartmann was born in Ohio and raised in California. He received a bachelor's degree in history from Stanford University, and a doctorate in English from the University of North Carolina at Chapel Hill. Currently an Associate Professor of English at Manhattanville College, in Purchase, New York, where he teaches literature and film studies, he lives in Norwalk, Connecticut. His poetry has been published in *Confluence, Confrontation, Enskyment.org, Inkwell, Red Wheelbarrow Magazine, WinningWriters, Pennsylvania English, Phi Kappa Phi Forum, Snake Nation, Texas Review*, and *The Worcester Review*. *Shiva Dancing* is his first book of poetry.

Photograph by Carol Caulfield.

www.ingramcontent.com/pod-product-compliance
Lightning Source LLC
LaVergne TN
LVHW041309080426
835510LV00009B/924